The Itch

Written by Adam and Charlotte Guillain

Rav and Asha were watching a film in Tess and Finn's flat.

"Is there any more popcorn?" asked Finn, his eyes glued to the screen.

"This bit's exciting!" whispered Asha.

Rav started to wriggle and scratch.

“I’m itchy,” he muttered.

“I feel tickly too!” said Tess. As she fidgeted, she knocked over the bowl of popcorn.

Finn stopped the film and went to get the dustpan and brush.

“What’s making us itch?” he asked, pulling up his shirt sleeve. “Have I got a rash?”

Asha shook her head.

Then Rav gulped. “Oh no!” he cried. “My mum said she got a letter from school about head lice! Do you think we’ve got them?”

Everyone squirmed and wriggled like worms as Tess yelled, “Dad!”

They stood in the kitchen while Mr Harrison checked their hair.

“No sign of any head lice!” he told them.

“Oh good!” said Asha. “But I’m still itchy.”

“Maybe you’re hot and that’s making you itchy. Why don’t you get some fresh air in the garden?” suggested Mr Harrison.

“Let’s take Skip with us,” said Tess. “I’ll put him back in his hutch.”

Tess checked Skip had plenty of food. Then she put fresh water in his bottle and some clean hay in the hutch.

Finn picked up a ball and threw it to Asha. "Catch!" he said.

But instead of catching it, Asha started scratching again.

“Sorry,” she muttered, picking up the ball and throwing it to Rav.

“Hang on!” cried Rav, scratching too.

"This is so annoying!" moaned Finn.

"Listen!" said Tess. "What's that rustling sound?"

"It's Skip!" cried Asha. "He's scratching too!"

"What's happening to us?" wailed Rav.

Tess ran indoors.

"Can we take Skip to the vet?" she asked her dad. "He's scratching too and he looks upset!"

Dad nodded. "Okay. Skip's due his yearly check-up anyway."

In the vet's waiting room, the friends wriggled and twitched. Even Mr Harrison started to scratch.

"This is miserable," he muttered.

"Please take Skip through," said the man at the desk.

The vet beckoned them all in with a smile.

"What can I do for you today?" she asked.

"Skip keeps scratching," cried Tess. "And so do we!"

The vet gently put Skip on the table and examined him.

"It's a simple problem," she said. "Skip's got fleas!"

Finn turned to his dad. "Fleas!" he squealed. "We've all been bitten by fleas!"

The vet told them how to treat Skip for fleas.

"You should wash your clothes and take baths to help stop the itching," she added.

Mr Harrison bought some spray for the carpets at home.

Back at the flats, Finn and Tess helped their dad on a massive cleaning mission. Then everyone had a bath.

While the carpets are drying, can we go to Rav's?

Good idea. I'll come too!

When they knocked on Rav's door, Mrs Joshi opened it.

"You might not want to come in," she said. "Alpa's come home from nursery with head lice!"

Mr Harrison stepped back.

“Would Rav like to come out with us?” he asked.

They knocked for Asha and headed to the bus stop.

"What would you like to see?" asked Finn and Tess's dad.

"*Bug Attack!*" said all four friends.

"Of course," sighed Mr Harrison and he went to buy the tickets.

Talk about the story

Answer the questions:

1 Where did they take Skip the rabbit?

2 Why was everyone itching?

3 Why did they have to clean the flat?

4 Why did Mr Harrison invite Rav to come out?

5 Why do pets have to have check-ups?

6 Have you ever been itchy? Did you find out why?

Can you retell the story in your own words?